# The Path to Restoration

## Finding Hope in the Midst of Brokenness

By Sarah Lowe

THE PATH TO RESTORATION

**First edition. December 8, 2019.**



ISBN: 979-8230683964

Written by Sarah Lowe.

The details of this book were based on Sarah's view of all that happened to her and not others' opinions.

This book is dedicated to my stepdad, Bryant Tickell, who passed away April of 2019. He always believed in me. He was one of the most giving men I know.

Thank you to my family and friends for helping me in this difficult time.

Thank you to Abba Father for getting me through, and the healing He's doing even now. He is why I wrote this book. He's always there for us, even when people let us down. He carried me through the dark nights of my soul.

Free gift: one of my songs

Visit www.oilywriter.wordpress.com[1] and fill out the message at the bottom to receive the free song video.

I also sell a CD of mine for $10.00 plus shipping and handling. Just email me on the wordpress site. Follow me on my facebook page called Encouragement with Sarah.

1. http://www.oilywriter.wordpress.com

Table of Contents

# Appendix A- How to receive Christ

Hi! Welcome to a sneak peak into my life. These words are pieces from my heart. I pray they encourage you and help you feel that you're not alone. I hope they inspire you and help you in the healing journey. Thank you for reading these words from my heart.

My Life

(written 2009)

She was born in Texas
A fat little babe
I guess she was happy
Until about the age of ten.
Her daddy left at age 12.
She was so sad
And mom held the bitterness in
And the girl held all this inside.
She felt so rejected.
She was teased at school.
She was not attractive.
She had very few friends.
At home she was miserable
She was mom to little sister
When she didn't know when Mom would be back.
She lived with cats
She took cold or no showers.
She was fearful at school
Because she smelled like poop.
She held onto Jesus.
He was her only hope.
He was so faithful.
His presence kept her going.
Many times she wanted death-
To be free of the pain.
But she knew that Christ died

So she'd live for Him.
The long-awaited day came
To move away to college.
She was so happy to be away that
The homesickness surprised her.
She almost had a boyfriend
but she was too young.
Besides, she told God
"No dating until I'm 20."
At 20, she was wanting
Her first boyfriend.
She had her eye on someone
So the friendship began.
The walks and talks were great.
Two years later they married.
She felt peace about it
Until her wedding day.
They really loved each other
But it was hard from the start.
This was not what she thought it'd be
But she tried to do her best.
The marriage wasn't working.
It was almost dead.
Three years later they separated
Then 16 months later, they divorced.
She cried when she saw him.
He'd been her best friend.
She knew it was over
And there's nothing she could do.
Twelve years earlier her
Parents had divorced.
The feeling of sadness and

Rejection came like a whoosh.
Would a man ever stay with her?
Would she die an old maid?
Only God could show her
The love and faithfulness she deserved.
This young girl was me.

# Chapter 1- Grief

Grief is tricky. It comes up at any time. You will think you are doing better, and then something sparks a memory and you cry. Most of my grief has been over relationships. My stepdad and grandmother have passed away. Much of my grief has been over losses of dreams as well. I've had half a dozen dreams be broken: 2 marriages, a career, a home, being a mom/having my own baby, and my parents' divorce. In the last year, I've had to grieve a home, a dog, a marriage, a couple friendships, stepdad passing, and in- laws. It's been the worst year of my life. But I know God will bring good out of it.

Grief scripture:

Job 5:11- He protects those who suffer.

Proverbs 14:13- Laughter can conceal a heavy heart, but when it ends, the grief remains.

Genesis 41:52- Joseph named his son Ephraim, for he said, "God has made me fruitful in the land of my grief.

Isaiah 54:6- The Lord has called you back from grief- as though you were a young wife abandoned by her husband," says your God.

Isaiah 53:3-He was despised and rejected- a man of sorrows, acquainted with deepest grief. We turned our backs on him and looked the other way. He was despised, and we did not care. (Jesus)

John 16:20b- You will grieve but your grief will suddenly turn to wonderful joy.

Here's a few tips when grieving:

1. Go to a support class. Griefshare is one I know of. Google it.
2. Use good music to help you. I have a station that is songs I like and songs that will cheer me up. It works. Worship, of course, has been invaluable to me.
3. Be with friends and family. Get involved in church. You need others. You can't do this alone.

We are meant for community.

4. Don't dwell on sadness but grieve some. It's a balance.
5. Pray a lot. God understands loss and grief. He can be your best friend through this.
6. Go do something that will make you laugh.
7. Be in the Word of God. Psalms is amazing when we are going through something difficult.
8. Self care. Guard your sleep and take care of yourself. I had to really guard my sleep and still do. Give yourself grace. You are going through a lot.

I hate when people tell me to move on. It's not helpful. Grief takes time-often longer than we want it to take.

Give yourself time and grace. You're doing great! God's with you-leading and healing you. I know because He's done it for me!

God bless.

<u>Bryant</u>

He's always been there.
He came just in time.
A constant one
He came when I was nine.
I used to resent him
Because he took my mom away
In the teenage years.
But hey,
she needed love. Okay?
The faithful neighbor
The kind man
He was full of smiles.
And he always would lend a hand.
He wasn't always around.
We did not live together.

But when there was a need
He was ready to help, indeed.
I loved him like a dad.
Cancer had taken over.
It was hard to watch it all.
This proud guy and tall.
This independent man
Was losing his fight.
Dad, Papa, Grandpa, too
Was going towards the light.
On his last day
He awoke just for me.
I was the last one to see him.
There we were-mom, siblings, and me.
He received Christ with a hand squeeze
And we praised the Lord.
His grace and mercy never end.
And all the angels roared.
God and he gave me that gift.
A day I'll never forget.
I told him I loved him
And said "goodbye Dad."

## Groot

5-11-19
I mostly raised him
I thought he was also mine.
He knew when I was sad.
He loved me at all times.
A Boston Terrier
A lot of energy

At the beginning not so fun
On the carpet he would pee
I was his mom
And never got to say goodbye.
What kind of dog dad does that?
Groot might as well have died.
I miss you puppy.
Always be a good boy
I hope he takes care of you
And you'll always have toys.
Goodbye
I love you.

---

<u>Gma</u>

5-11-19
Gma was some lady.
In each room she brought joy.
She taught me so much.
I felt loved with her touch.
She never complained
Even with a broken back.
She led a positive life.
I never saw her in strife.
Skip Bo was the game
We would play for hours.
She kept us laughing always
Even on gloomy days.
She was short but mighty-
Never hesitated to dance.
"Chew 40 times" she'd say,
And she always made my day.

I love you Gma Shirley
My Sunshine

---

Loss

5-11-19
The losses are high
The pain is unbearable.
I've lost people, dog,
And material things.
I've lost the in-laws
Their smiles, love, and giving.
I've lost friends
Who have taken his side
I've lost a home
That was mine 5 years.
My first home I ever had-
So hard to let go.
I've lost two husbands.
I wanted them to last.
They made their choices
Best friends now part of the past.

Broken Dreams

Hmmm...where do I start
I have at least eight.
At the beginning, I'll start.
My dad first broke my heart.
I can't rightly discern why
There' so much hurt.
But he did leave and

I've never felt good enough.
I dream of 50 year anniversary
Staying long time with the same man.
No, it didn't happen.
Two men from me ran.
My first home
Kids were supposed to fill it.
Infertility stung
My mom dream is in the pit.
I worked 13 years
For a career that is now void.
I don't understand this loss
I'm really sad and annoyed.
I know my calling now
And it took some time.
But I can't fulfill it now.
Fostering is my dream.

---

<u>I'm No Mom</u>

2019
I've worked with kids since 16
They bless me so.
I hoped to be a mom by 25.
But I'm 38 and still waiting, you know.
I don't understand
Why I get so much rain.
I try not to compare
But I'm tired of the pain.
They post about their babies.
They post about their life.
Here I am -stuck.

I'm not even a wife.
I trust you, God,
Though I don't understand.
A kid won't solve everything,
But they are like arrows in the hand.

Lost Love

Thank you for your unconditional love.
The meaning of love is lost in this earth,
But you convey the true meaning that comes from above.
In my eyes, you have much worth.
Your love is sweeter than honey.
When I have a bad day,
You always make me laugh by doing something funny.
You make me feel better right away.
You turn my fear into joy.
You help me see myself differently.
Although I think of you as just a boy,
Ill never forget the love you gave me.
Now it's time for me to move on.
But please don't forget me while I'm gone.
(To Austin-1998)
Sarah Martin

---

Not Alone

She sits alone in a crowd.
She feels lonely.
Only God knows her thoughts.
What a place to be.
A widow sits alone

In an empty house
Grieving over her loss-
Tears streaming down her cheeks.
Oh, lovely daughter
I see the pain
But know I'm here
You are not alone
Not alone
A young girl
Stares out the window.
Her husband has gone.
The divorce makes her want to die.
Oh, lovely daughter
I see the pain.
But know I'm here.
You are not alone.
Not alone.

---

Letting Go

(After my divorce)
4-28-10
I'm good at loving others.
I'm good at giving my all.
But when it comes to letting go,
I'm not good at that at all.
I put up my walls
because of fear of getting hurt.
I might as well let them in,
Cause either way life's gonna hurt.
I'm letting go of the past
Letting go of the pain

Letting go of the fake love
to have open hands for the real thing.
I'm good at holding onto pain-
good at recounting the hurt.
I choose to forgive
and find healing for my heart.
I let go
Of the life I lived with him
I let go
Of the love I have for him.

Bow the Knee

I had a typical working day.
Everything was going okay.
Then I heard the horrible news.
All my kids were crushed and dead.
Still in shock from the first part
I had a heavy heart.
And I heard my animals were gone.
They were taken and some of them died.
When I thought nothing else could go wrong,
God took all my joyful song.
I got spots of leprosy.
The physical pain was unbearable.
God, what have I done?
Why all this misery?
I don't understand at all
But I will gladly bow the knee.
God gives and takes away
Blessed be His name
My wife said curse God and die.

My friends said I must've sinned.
No one offered me any hope.
But God vindicated me, and my heart did mend.
I got two times as much back:
Ten kids, three thousand animals and clean skin.
God is good and can be trusted.
Regardless of what men say- even my own kin.
God, what have I done?
Why all this misery?
I don't understand at all.
But I will gladly bow the knee.

## Turn to the Lord

My heart broke and bled.
I just want to be held.
Who can I turn to?
My home's a lonely place.
Painful memories in every space.
Where can I go?
My love walked out the door
Now I am poor.
What am I going to do?
Getting out of bed's a chore.
I don't want to live anymore.
When will the pain end?
I turn to the Lord.
I fall at the cross.
I'll keep living
There's life after loss.
I don't understand how this can be Your plan.
Why is this happening?

God can take my questions.
He doesn't answer why.
But this too shall pass,
And my tears He will dry.
You gotta turn to Him.
He will never leave us.
He is faithful and true.
So, turn to the Lord.

Things People Say

People mean well
But boy-they don't know.
What to say to you grieving
Like "just let it go".
"You're better off
Don't be sad
Get over it.
It's not that bad."
"You're being a baby.
Just move on, my friend.
I know the storm is raging,
But just forget the wind."
I forgive them.
They know not what they d0.
They really try to help.
Just give them grace anew.

Will you Be Jesus?

5-16-10
My scar is grief.
My spouse died last year.
I miss him so,

and all I have left are tears.
My scar is loneliness
and I feel no one cares.
I feel all alone,
and it's almost too much to bear.
My scar is sickness,
and I've lost my will to live.
I'm in so much pain.
What can you give?
Will you be Jesus to me?
Come and stay awhile.
Will you be Jesus to me?
Will you go the extra mile?
We all have scars
But remember me.

If the Walls Could Talk

If the walls could talk
They'd tell you of my pain.
The many nights I cried
Myself to sleep from neglect.
They'd tell you about
The rage and fits;
Hurtful words spoken.
The brokenness started from day one.
They'd tell you all the times
He chose porn over me.
And the time he cheated on me
While it was still my house and bed.
He'd defiled the marriage bed
Which God does not take lightly.

"Vengeance is mine", says the Lord,
"For hurting my baby girl."
If the walls could talk
You'd hear about the slander
To my precious God.
His accusations to a holy God.
They'd tell you about
The lying and the yelling,
The name calling,
And verbal abuse.
They'd tell you
how I took care of him
but he beat me down emotionally-
Made me want to die.
The walls would say how I felt-
So alone and lonely.
I felt like low priority to him.
He didn't deserve the title "husband".
You'd hear about the blaming,
Gaslighting, and spending.
Thousands of dollars spent
Behind my back
===========================

Are You Here?

3-9-19
Oh God
Are you here?
I need to know you're near.
Please take all my fear.
Are you here?

You seem distant.
I know you're not.
I need you now.
I need you a lot!
I know they aren't true
But the lies circle me.
"God's left you.
He's holding out on you."
Please speak
Let your words resound.
Let the pain, hurt and fear
All fall to the ground.
You have the power.
I don't understand.
But trust you, I must.
Just please hold my hand.

Grief questions

1.What have you had to grieve?

2.What have you lost? It's important to identify them all.

3.Are you letting yourself grieve so you can heal and move on?

4.What promise are you hanging onto? In my first divorce, I stood on Hebrews 13:5- I will never leave you or forsake you. (God)

This year it's been Romans 8:28. "And ALL things work together for good of those that love God and are called to His purpose."

# Chapter 2- Anger

Intro

I don't consider myself an angry person, but circumstances have made it come out lately in me. It really scared me. I sought help because it was new territory for me. During childhood, I had reasons to be angry, but I stuffed those feelings. I stuffed them for 22 years ya'll. At 22 when I first got married, the anger started surfacing. I didn't understand where it was coming from, but now I do.

Most of us either stuff or blast our feelings. I'm a stuffer. It's not good for our health to be a stuffer. It's not good for other people or relationships when we blast and yell it out. It hurts others. We must learn to let the anger go in a healthy way. Anger is usually not wrong. It's a natural response to when something is unjust or hurts us. We should be angry when treated wrong or when God's laws are broken. The Bible says, "Be angry and sin not. Do not let the sun go down on your anger."

When I was cheated on and my ex put a woman in my house, I've never felt so much anger. How dare he? It was total disrespect to me. I don't give my heart easily or my sex life to someone easily. And this husband gave it away to some random person. For two weeks I couldn't sleep because I kept thinking of them together. I know of no worse betrayal. I had trouble sleeping for almost 3 months when I found a different girl living in my house.

Anger and depression are connected. About a week after I was told about the cheating, I got super angry. The first half of the day I lashed out at him in anger. (Wrong way to deal with it, by the way.)

But that night, oh God. I've never been so depressed. I wanted to end it all. I went to a friend's party and just sat in the corner watching them play games. Inside, I didn't care about anything. I wanted the pain to end. I wanted some relief. I wouldn't have killed myself, but I've never been that down about life. Like my sister said, "No man is worth your life."

I put it in a friend Facebook group- "Would anyone care if I wasn't here anymore?" That's a cry for help ya'll. At 11:30 at night three friends showed up at my door, worried about me. I appreciate that more than I can express.

Scripture on anger:

Ephesians 4:26-27- Do not sin by letting anger control you. Don't let the sun go down on your anger.

James 1:14- You must be quick to listen, slow to speak, and slow to get angry.

Proverbs 29:11- Fools vent their anger, but the wise quietly hold it back.

Romans 12:9- Dear friends, never take revenge. Leave that to the righteous anger of God. For scripture says- "I will take revenge; I will pay them back," says the Lord.

Psalm 4:4- Don't sin by letting anger control you. Think about it overnight and remain silent.

Anger tips:

1. Choose forgiveness. Say it aloud, "I forgive you for..." as many times as the anger comes up. "I forgive you and I let you go," also helps me. You won't feel like forgiving. It's a choice and it gets easier with time. It's real difficult at first, especially if the person hurt you really bad. This is the only way to get truly free of anger. Forgiveness is for you. A lot of times the person who hurt us couldn't care less if we forgive them or not.
2. Exercise
3. Keep giving it to God. Vengeance is His. Remember that. God will do a much better job than you and I could. Remember that we've sinned against God way more than we could sin against each other.
4. Find a healthy outlet. It could be exercise, crafting, or a new hobby...

5. Talk it out with someone but don't tell too many people. Be conscious of how much you talk about it. Counseling is great because it's an outside person who you can share anything with.

---

Where's Loyalty

1997-1998

(I wrote this after a classmate got charged with killing.)

I had never loved a man. I had learned to guard my heart.

All men seemed like scum. My Dad was the first to show me that part.

He cheated on me. He stabbed me in the back.

He cheated on me. I'll never get close to anyone again.

Then I met a man at work.

I thought I could let my guard down.

He wasn't the person I thought he was.

I found that out on this dark night in the town.

I asked, "Why'd you do this to me?"

He said, "I'm sorry. Give me another try."

I said, "I never should've trusted you. No, I won't because you make me cry."

Who can you trust in this world when your friend turns his back on you?

Tell me, when people do you wrong,

What should you do?

Love has gone out the window.

I want to get it back,

But I won't risk getting hurt again.

I'm glad the Lord has everything I lack.

Unseen Snake

5-19-19

When I look back at my life

I see good and bad.
God did a lot,
But I see an unseen snake.
That unseen snake
Wants us to focus on people.
Get bitter, angry, and mad
Starting with mom and dad.
"It's all their fault"
He whispers.
"Pay them back for the pain.
Think of what you would you would gain."
That unseen snake
Is a lying thief.
He comes only to destroy.
Don't let him take your joy.
He stole my marriages.
He took my joy.
He caused us poverty
I'm onto his ploy.
Do not trust the unseen snake.
He watches and lurks
Waiting for a weak moment.
No worries. God's much greater than the jerk!

<u>Anger</u>

Anger-It scares me
More than depression
To feel so much rage
What is the key?
I wanted to hit him
And his girlfriend too.

I wanted to smash their cars
To pieces, like jars.
But anger unleashed
Is never a good idea.
It does nothing good.
Remember- do what you should.
I wanted to hold him hostage
For the hurt, to make him pay.
But Jesus wouldn't do that
"I forgive you," He'd say.
We have to forgive.
It's the only good way.
As we do it more and more,
It gets easier- we see a new day.
Workouts, busyness, distractions
May help for a time.
But only in letting go,
True peace we will know.

## Hate the Devil

5-19-19
Don't hate
The man who hurt you,
The woman who left-
Under the sun, nothing new
Hate the devil.
Don't hate
The lying cheaters
The idiot people
We all do wrong-Look at Peter
Hate the devil.

Don't hate
All the lost souls
Hurting so many people
Full of horrible goals
Hate the devil.
Hate the world.
Hate the devil.
Hate the sin and evil.
But never hate a person.
Hate the devil.

## The Real Enemy

5-20-19
(help of friends)
Manipulation, lying
Hate, deception
Who is under all these?
The real enemy
Cheating, stealing
Disrespect, lack of love
Violence and crime
The real enemy
Abuse, heart breaker, envy
Rape and murder
Jealousy, rage, and selfishness
There are not from the Father.
I'm angry to be hurt.
I don't understand
How someone can be so mean.
It seems they get away with it
But they are seen.

They are seen by God.
The devil is the real enemy.
======================================

Justice Be Served

Anger
Rage
Betrayal to the core
That's how I feel
I've never been so angry
It scares me.
I want to hate him
And that's not me.
It's so not fair.
He gets what he wants.
He hurts me
And moves on like he doesn't care.
I'm angry.
I don't deserve this.
It feels he's getting away with sin.
Help me trust you, Lord.
You're my vindication, God.
I want to hurt him
Like he's hurt me.
He's given me hell for years.
Vindicate me, God.
Let justice be served.
Oh Church
2019
I was born and raised in a Texas church.
I'm glad I grew up Christian.

But the pain inflicted
Oh Church
They acted better than us
We were just poor.
To them, we weren't good enough.
My mom had it rough.
Oh Church
How do you think judgment
Will bring people in?
It's supposed to be a hospital
Not a party for the rich or cool
Oh Church
A Christian boss watched me like a hawk.
She judged my every move
And then fired me.
Gave Christians a bad name, you see.
Oh Church
Guard yourself against self -righteousness
Jesus rebuked those people.
An accusing tongue is not godly.
Oh Church, can't you see.
Repent on your knees.
Love is the key.
Porn
2019
Porn makes me angry.
These women make me mad.
They sell themselves
With no thought of the damage had.
It is a strong sin.
It seems to grab a hold.
Porn distorts their thinking.

To their wife, they become cold.
Love vs. lust
I want the first one.
Making love is sweet
It shouldn't be bam and were done.
So many marriages breaking
This fake sex causes pain.
It hurts families.
The damage remains.
I Deserve More
(Written 2019 about first husband)
He just up and left
Just like my dad.
No respect for marriage.
It made me very sad.
I was angry.
There was no good reason.
He just decided to quit
Right before the holiday season.
You trust someone.
You give all your heart.
You stay committed.
They don't give a fart.
It seems like everyone
Either leaves in body or mind.
A faithful, loving man
Is quite hard to find.
The lying makes me angry.
The trust goes out the door.
The devil is father of lies.
From a man I deserve more.
Judgmental Eyes

2019
I feel judged
And it's not something made up.
These once close friends
empty my emotional cup.
They don't understand my pain.
They don't have a clue
how painful divorce is.
Can I hide in my shoes?
I've not done everything right.
I've used things to cope.
It took six months
before I had any hope.
You're not the judge.
Judgmental remarks make me mad
You were a close friend.
Another loss that makes me sad.
People-don't be self- righteous.
You're no better than anyone else.
Righteous in Christ alone
We all mess up.
You can love and not condone.
Worthy of Love
2019
I don't deserve abuse.
I'm a good person.
I deserve to be encouraged.
It makes me want to run.
Yes, I did leave,
But emotionally falling apart.
He just said whatever he wanted.
Another man that broke my heart.

A husband knows what hurts
What will tear us down.
The words of accusation
go in my head 'round and 'round.
You're worthy, too, my friend.
No man or woman can define your worth.
Reject those lies.
You've been precious since birth.
Sad Song
2019
(Event happened in 2008)
We were best friends
And roommates, too.
She bounced a check.
Lots of money was due.
I could've been homeless
many times without my family.
She never paid me back.
I had to make her pack.
It took a long time
to forgive her.
It really hurt me-
Not even one "sorry".
She didn't mean to
but she handed it wrong.
My first best friend
Joyful music turned to sad song.

## Chapter 2 Personal anger questions

1. What injustices have made you angry?

2. How did you deal with it? Did you respond in a right way?
3. Have you worked through the anger? How?
4. Are you a stuffer or a yeller?
5. Forgiveness is the best way. Have you been choosing that and working through it?

Forgiveness steps:

1. Determine who is it and what they did.
2. Say aloud, "I forgive (name) for (what they did). I release you from my judgment."
3. Do it every time anger or sadness comes up because of it.
4. Having someone do a roll play with you can be even more powerful.
5. Choose forgiveness. Especially at the beginning you won't feel like it. It's a choice.

# Chapter 3- Depression

Depression is a beast. I don't even believe I have clinical depression, but I have had my share. Clinical depression is the worst. That's what my ex had. You need constant counseling and meds. Clinical means something is not working right in the brain.

Depression is also a sign that something is wrong. (even if it's not clinical). Our bodies are trying to tell us that something is wrong in our heart and emotions. It can be because of disobeying God. It can be because of not working through our feelings correctly. It can be just because someone does us wrong. It can be because of a loss.

Depression scripture:

Psalm 42

Ecclesiastes 7:3- Sorrow is better than laughter for sadness has a refining influence on us.

Psalm 119:28- I weep with sorrow; encourage me by Your word.

Here's some tips that help me:

1.Be social. Read the Word of God. Meditate on the Word of God.

2.Be around believers. Don't isolate yourself. (The devil did that to me when I was a teenager so I'm aware of this scheme.) A single sheep is defenseless against a wolf, but a pack ensures safety. We become the top five people that we hang around.

3.Allow yourself to feel it enough but not too much. (It's a delicate balance.) You may start off needing an hour to cry a day and end by needing only 5 minutes if some pain comes up.

4. Watch what you put into your mind-movies, songs, etc. They affect your mood.

5.Pray. In my darkest, worst nights, God got me through. It was Him alone that was there and helped me. He's always there and listening. Thank you Abba!

6.Get into counseling. Someone with a broken arm would seek a doctor. It should be the same with a broken heart, mind, or emotions.

Go to an emotional doctor. My counselors helped me a lot! Outside perspective is so key to healing.

7.Use music. Worship was invaluable for me. Many days that's how I got through.

8.Up your self care. Shower, exercise, eat, and sleep daily. Get enough sleep. I had to really guard my sleep because emotional traumas take 70-80% of our energy. That's how much energy is put on emotions. Love yourself well.

9.Help someone else. When I asked my facebook friends what helps them, this was a common answer. It gets our eyes off our own pain and to help others.

10. I used to be a person that journaled often but got out of the habit. But toward the end of my divorce, journaling was invaluable. It really helps get the emotions out. Trapped emotions will cause us problems. It's a matter of time.

11.Get around loving friends and family. They are there to support you, listen, and just be there. Someone just being with me made a big difference for me.

12. A young, but wise, friend said to be thankful. Oh yes, sister! It's important. It keeps our focus on the good because there's always lots to be thankful for; even in the midst of grief, loss, pain, and depression.

13. Go talk to a trusted friend or family member.

14. Go do something you love. Fun is a hard thing for me. It doesn't come naturally these days. I have to plan it for it to happen. I love to dance, read, sing, do crafts, watch movies, and go bowling. I love to watch the sun set. What do you love? Make a list.

January 2

(This was written in high school. Boy, I thought I knew it all.)
I was chosen to be in this family
If I would've had to choose, I would've said no.
Someone else chose for me to live.
If I knew what was ahead of me, when I was born,
I never would've come out of my mother's womb.
All my life others have made choices for me.
My mom and dad decided to have me.
My mom decided what I would wear and eat.
They decided where I would live and go to school.
Other's decided which teachers I'd have.
Teachers chose the material I would learn.
The only choices I had to make were the following:
Do my school work or don't do it.
Live or die.
Live with God or without God.
I chose to do my school work,
Live,
And live with God.
Now I'm starting to have more choices to make.
It's hard to start making your own decisions.
I hope I don't make the bad mistakes my parents made.
I feel like a prisoner in my own house.
I can leave, but where can I go.
There's no safe hiding place to get away.
Only a cold world that offers no help.
No one has seen all the tears that I've cried.
Except for my heavenly Father up above.
No one but He was there to comfort me
When I felt all alone.
I listened to a tape when I was younger

I fell and my sister asked, "Are you okay?"
I replied, "I always don't cry."
I wish I could still say that today.
I took a walk yesterday around the neighborhood.
There were people outside because it was a pretty day.
But none of them even cared to say hello.
I felt like I was invisible- not to be seen.
I could still see them though-
Carrying on with their tasks.
A teenage girl chasing a teenage boy,
A man outside with his boat,
A little boy and two teenagers on the lawn;
A family outside helping to get a truck connected to something
A little boy riding his bike,
Two little boys walking and talking together.
Finally, I saw 3 children playing together.
A little boy said, "I'm going home."
When I saw a little girl I thought,
"I wish I could be a little girl again."
Childhood is the best part of life.
NO worries or cares,
NO responsibilities on hand.
The freedom to sleep, eat and play all day.
I'm approaching my senior year.
I'm scared but I want to go.
I want to go to SAGU and
Meet the man of my dreams.
If I wasn't allowed to dream
I'd be in trouble.
Dreaming is always there to do
When the real world seems to be crushing you.
Has the world become better or worse?

Even though there' s no war, there's battles in
Homes all over the world.
I say it's worse because family is important.
Family used to be all you needed.
Now there's kids looking elsewhere for their needs.
All the problems that this country has is about family.
Gangs, violence, drugs...
How would it be today if Eve had said, "No"?
It would be a perfect society, a utopia.
Sin is what destroys people.
I thank God that he forgives all who ask Him.
There was a sin I did when I was younger.
When I asked for forgiveness,
I felt such a cleansing forgiveness.
I no longer feel convicted of what I had done.
What's happened to family values?
Women get pregnant before they're married.
Adults drink alcohol until they are sick.
People turn to drugs to escape life's heartaches.
When they should be turning to Jesus.
People get married just for the fun of it.
It's hard to find something clean to watch on TV.
Money and wealth look good to us
But it can't fill the emptiness in our hearts.
Divorce occurs more and more.
(I'm not judging. Obviously, I'm in that boat too.)
People think about killing themselves.
Fathers neglect providing for their families.
God gave us rules for our own good.
But many times we choose not to listen,
So our lives become chaos and destruction.
Obey God because He knows what He's saying.

He's There

April 24,2010
Everyone has left.
No one is faithful to me.
I feel so alone.
God, did you leave me, too?
When you can't see Him, He's there.
When you can't feel Him, He's there.
When you can't hear Him, he's there.
You've gotta believe- Jesus is there.
No one seems to love me. No one seems to care.
I feel nothing good. God's love, are you still there?
I pray and cry out to God, but He is silent still. I need His voice of truth.
I want to do His will.
Believe He's there
When your senses tell you no.
Believe He cares
When all else says He don't.

Mirror Image

4-12-96
When I look in the mirror,
What do I see?
I see sadness through my face.
I see me.
My green eyes look back at me with sorrow.
I can hear them say:
"When will the tears cease?
Will we cry today?"
My big nose longs to smell something sweet,
But I don't have a sweet scent to give my nose.

It wonders: "When will I smell flowers again?"
I say, "When all the rain stops, you can smell a rose."
My pretty lips want to smile,
but my mind disagrees.
My dry mouth wants good food,
But you can't get honey without bees.
My forehead sticks out too far.
It shines because of the oil on my skin.
The acne reminds me that I am still a teen.
I can never win!
My long face has a few freckles.
My sister says they are angel kisses.
If only they would take away my acne,
They would fulfill one of my greatest wishes.
Why are looks so important?
I would rather be happy.
Happiness means more to me
Than whether I look nappy.

Put your Value

Men may leave but Jesus won't.
The man stands there as you cry.
Jesus gives you peace and hugs you.
The man just says goodbye.
Do not put your value in
What men say.
Put your value in
The price Jesus paid- His life.
Men may ignore you and not love.
But God's love is forever.
He sees every tear and cares.

Men may not commit to forever.
Men may say hurtful words.
But Jesus speaks love, life, and hope.
God will never bring up your past.
He forgives us, so with life we can cope.
A man can never satisfy.
He cannot meet your needs
Only in Jesus is true love.
This love is all you need.

Worst Night Ever

I've had my share of depression.
Depression is often for me.
But that terrible night
For my life, it was a fight.
He told me about the cheating.
Anger was there for sure.
I was not expecting
The worst depression I've ever known.
They say anger
Is depression locked inside.
September 8 I had a lot.
The world grew dim to rot.
Would anyone care
If I went to heaven?
I reached out to friends
And 3 came to my aide.
(showed up at my door)
I sat at a party
Despairing of life
They laughed while I wanted to scream

It was the end of a dream.

---

Not Forgotten

2009
She sees couples together
She remembers her own
Time when she had someone.
Now she's all alone.
She works for the Lord.
She gives her all.
Longing for recognition
But feeling invisible.
Almighty God says
"You're not forgotten.
You've gotta trust me-
I'm working all for good though you can't see it.
Trust me."
She cries to God
"I feel forgotten.
When is my breakthrough?
When will the waiting be a has been?"
Almighty God says
"You're not forgotten.
You've gotta trust me-
I'm working all for good though you can't see it.
Trust me."

Forgotten

5-16-19
I know feeling forgotten.

I know heart pain.
I know feeling brushed aside
And feeling like I'm insane.
Has God forgotten me?
I know He has not.
How does a Father forget
A child He has blood bought?
Friends and family seem too busy.
No time to help me out.
I feel a void I cannot fill.
They just have lives, no doubt.
Even at work, I feel left out.
Faithful I am for five years.
Others get all the breaks.
I just get tears.
Forgotten by my ex
He's so good at moving on.
It feels like a death.
No contact so it's like he's gone.
===================================

Hiding place
2009
My heart broke and bled. I just wanted to be held.
Who can I turn to?
My home was a lonely place
Painful memories in every space.
Where can I go?
My love walked out the door
Now I am poor
What am I going to do?

Getting out of bed's a chore.
I don't want to live anymore.
When will the pain end?
I don't understand.
How can this be your plan?
Why is this happening?
You protect me from trouble.
You are my hiding place.
You surround me with songs of deliverance.
You are my hiding place.

Job

April 11,2010

I loathe my life and speak in bitterness of soul. Do not condemn me God.

Does it please You to oppress me with a rod?
Why did I not die before birth?
My days are almost gone.
Turn away so I can have joy.
Before I descend to a dark void.
Oh, that God would grant what I hope for- that He would crush me.
But the joy in the pain is that I did not deny His name.
My eyes are dim with grief.
My frame is but a shadow.
My plans are shattered apart,
And so are the desires of my heart.

---

It was Mine

2-2-19

It was my house

For five years.
Someone taking over
Is my fear.
I planted the yellow flowers.
I cleaned it.
I lived life there.
On the couches, did I sit.
Oh, if the walls could talk
They'd talk of tears.
They saw my pain.
Wailing did they hear.
I've got to let go.
It's so very hard.
The pain is not worth a house.
My heart I will guard.
He was my husband.
That was my bed.
That was my kitchen.
The dog I fed.
It's not fair that someone
Can hurt me so bad.
He made dumb choices
That made me so sad.

# Chapter 3- depression questions

1. Is your depression clinical or situational or both?
2. When did your depression hit? (age)
3. How are you dealing with it?
4. What lies are causing some depression?
5. What truths do you need to write and say aloud often?
6. Which of the suggestions above are you going to try?

# Chapter 4 -Joy

As I type this on June first, I have finally had more good days the last two weeks. It was 1-2 good days a week. But now it's only 1-2 bad days a week. That is progress. I'll take it. Joy! There's nothing like it. It makes you feel alive and free. It encourages the soul.

The joy of the Lord is your strength. That's what the Bible says.

Been feeling much joy lately? If the answer is no, it's okay. Just know that if you are doing everything you can toward healing, joy will return. Feeling weak or strong lately? Either way, it's okay. Just don't let the enemy take your joy.

Scriptures on joy:

Galatians 5:22- The fruit of the Spirit is love, joy, peace, patience...

Romans 12:12- Be joyful in hope.

Prov.10:28-The prospect of the righteous is joy.

Psalm 16:11- You fill me with joy in your presence and eternal pleasures at your right hand.

Isaiah 55:12- You WILL go out with joy and be led forth with peace.

Isaiah 51:11-Those who have been ransomed by the Lord will return. They will enter Jerusalem singing, crowned with everlasting joy. Sorrow and mourning will disappear, and they will be filled with joy and gladness.

Joy Tips:

1. Realize that joy is different from happiness. Happiness is based on circumstance. Joy is not. We can choose joy despite bad circumstance. This however does not mean we don't have to feel or work through the pain.
2. Realize that God never promised an easy life or that all our dreams would come true. Broken dreams will happen. He promises we will have trouble in this life. Hebrews 11 is known as the faith chapter and here is a key scripture. "They died not

seeing the promise come to pass." That actually brought freedom to me. All His promises are not guaranteed this side of heaven.

3. It won't be horrible forever. This too shall pass.
4. If our joy goes, our strength goes. So do whatever necessary to keep the joy alive.
5. Find joy in the little things: a sunny day, a car starting, a sweet friend, a child's smile...There's always something to be thankful for. Find those things.

2-12-11

Sit at My feet

The world is hustle bustle
Busy running to and fro.
It leaves you tired and empty
It won't help you grow.
Sit at my feet. Feel my love.
Listen to my voice. Find the rest you need.
Work and people yelling your name- so much louder than my voice.
I speak softly as a gentleman.
Who you listen to is your choice.
Come to me for the rest, peace, truth, and love you need.
I want your heart more than your deeds.
I'm not in the thunder.
I'm not in the storm. I'm not in the fire.
I am the still small voice. Listen to me child.

Jesus

Jesus- no ordinary name tells us much of who He is
Immanuel-God with us
Savior of His people
He is Jesus
Bread of Life
To nourish our hungry souls.
Living water
To quench our thirsty souls.
Resurrection
To breathe new life when we feel dead.
Life-abundant and eternal
He's the lifter of our heads.
Jesus is the light of the world.
Beaming light in our dark lives
The way to walk toward life
The truth that cannot hide

Let me Come

I am the Holy Spirit
A deposit of what is to come.
I'll live inside you
If you will let me come.
I will never leave you.
I will never part.
I speak truth to you.
You can trust me with your heart.
I am gentle.
I am kind.
I'm not like men, you see.
Let me ease your mind.

I can be your Best Friend.
I can feel your pain.
I cry when you cry.
I comfort you in the rain.
I will refresh
I will bring you peace
If you let me come

---

Go Home

2010
I just wanna go home
To try my true love
Where there's no rain.
God won't hurt me in pain.
My true love is God alone.
He alone satisfies. I want to look into His eyes.
I wanna see His face
Dance for a while
Be held by Him
To touch and be with Him
I have the hope of heaven
When life gets me down.
NO more pain or tears
NO more endless fears
I'll praise you forever
MY eternal friend.

I Choose Joy

7-13-10
Though my heart aches today

I choose joy.
Though the past haunts my present
I choose joy.
I choose joy when life is not so good.
I choose joy because God says I should.
Though I feel all alone
I choose joy.
Though it seems no one cares
I choose joy.
There's something I can't see.
There's a breakthrough coming for me.
Lord, help me to wait.
To trust you and get on my knees

I Understand

A Christmas song by Sarah Lowe
12-19-10
The Father came to me- said,
"Son it's time to go
Go save the world
so us they can know."
I am your High Priest.
I was broken for you.
You can come to me
'cause I've been there too.
I understand.
People were expecting a great King
coming on His throne.
But when I came,
I came as a baby alone.
I know the growing pains

and the hurt of rejection.
I understand life's trials
and the struggle with temptation.

<u>I Love You Lord</u>

3-8-11
I love you Lord. You're so good to me
I love you Lord. You're better than I could ever be.
I love you in the morning when the sun comes over the horizon.
I love you at noon when there's much work to be done.
I love you in the evening when the moon and stars come out.
I love you all day long. You're with me- no doubt.
I love you all day long when stress comes my way.
I love when you're near. I need you every hour of every day.

<u>Who do you Listen to?</u>

2009
They say-make lots of money
But God is my Provider.
A man's life doesn't consist of abundance of things. They say- do whatever you want.
But I know there will be a judgment day.
We will be judged for our words and our actions.
Who do you listen to of the voice in your mind?
Jesus, the world, or the devil
Only in Jesus, truth you'll find.
They say get lots of pleasure but only God satisfies.
I gotta do His will. They say you need power.
But I say God's all powerful.
I don't need to be in control.

They say- take without giving.
But Jesus said, "It's more blessed to give."
Life's not all about me.
They say- go to lots of doctors
But I know God is my Healer.
By His stripes I am healed.
The world is a liar.
The devil is a liar.
You can even lie to yourself.
But Jesus is the way, truth, and life.

The Good Shepherd

2009
The Lord cares for me. He meets my needs.
He protects me from danger. I follow where He leads.
He grants me peaceful rest. He brings restoration.
Even in a dark valley, I will not fear destruction.
He is Emmanuel- God with us. He draws me near.
He drives away my enemies. I am comforted when His voice I hear.
My enemies see His favor on me.
He satisfies my soul.
His anointing covers me.
My Abba makes me whole.
He loves me. He's good to me.
All of my earthly life, I will be with Him for eternity.

Give me a Dream

Give me a dream. A dream that's straight from You. Give me a dream-
a dream that's too big for me.

I put you in boxes and try to say what you can't do.
My faith is small but there's nothing you can't do.
This life is empty without your purpose.
I don't want to just survive. I want to be victorious.
Dreams of marriage and kids cannot fill that void.
I say no status quo. Use me and fill me with joy.
Oh Lord, I need you More than breath.
Lord come, because no vision brings death.

Ask and receive

He knows every bird -the field creatures are His.
He's got all the money you need. He said to test Him in this.
Ask and receive. God has it all. What do you need?
All you have to do is call.
The world belongs to Him-All that is in it. God Almighty is His name.
So don't you dare quit.
You may need provision, healing, or peace.
Your problem looks so great,
But to Him it's so small.
You just have to wait.

---

So Beautiful

4-28-10
You are so beautiful inside and out.
I cannot lie, you see. I mean every word.
When you look in the mirror I know what you see.
You see ugliness and pain. I see beauty and healing.
When you worry about what others think
You've given them the place of me. It only matters what I think.

Even when your hair's a mess and makeup is running down your cheeks.
I see straight to the heart- a heart that my face seeks.
Your daddy didn't affirm your beauty when you needed it most.
But I wish you could see how I see you the most.

Times of testing

5-22-10
I came with my son.
I didn't know what God had in mind.
I brought no sacrifice.
He tested me to see if I'd give up mine.
I lost many things dear to me.
My children, health and money
I didn't understand and stood in grief.
But I trusted God when life was far from funny.
We spent 40 years in the desert.
We complained about the conditions.
But in this journey, when we wanted slavery instead
We learned to trust and depend on God and His mission.
God tests to see what's in our heart.
Sometimes we pass the test.
Other times we fail miserably
But God changes us to be our best.
When we run to Him
He changes us for the best.

Psalm 17

Show the wonder of your love
For those who take refuge in you.

Keep me as the apple of your eye.
Protect me- You know why.
I have kept your ways
Not turning right or left.
God, I call on you.
You will answer me, too.
Hear me God.
I do not lie.
You can test me.
Faithful I will be.
My enemies surround me.
Hard hearted and speaking with arrogance;
Like a lion hungry for prey.
Lord, rescue me from them today.
These men have only this life.
You provide for our needs and future generations.
In righteousness I'll see your face.
I'll be satisfied seeing your face.

## I Think

2010
(what God thinks)
I think you are precious.
I think you are kind.
I think you are beautiful.
I think you are mine.
I think you are priceless.
I think you are sweet.
I think you are good enough.
I think you are neat.
I think you are loving.

I think you're wise, too.
I think you are worth it.
And I know I love you.
I know you better than anyone else.
I see all the good and bad.
I love and accept you just the same.
I'm your everlasting Dad.
======================================

The Most
5-9-10
I love a sunset
Over a gorgeous ocean.
I love the mountains
And the clouds in motion.
I love a beautiful spring day
With birds chirping happily.
I love eating chocolate
With someone I love dearly.
I love God discussions
And worshipping the King.
I Love being with Him
And this is why I sing.
But I love Jesus the most-
More than any earthly good.
I Love Jesus the most
And not just because I should.
=================================

Grace
5-23-10
It's His grace

That I am here.
It's His grace
That takes the fear.
It's His grace.
The thorn in my side
The weakness in me.
It doesn't feel good
But It's humbling me.
Daily life gets me down
The job is so hard.
The father's carrying me.
His favor surrounds me like a guard.
Depression comes around.
Discouragement wants to bring me down.
Don't think about the lies or past.
They will only make me frown.
It's His grace
That I am here.
It's His grace
That takes the fear.
It's His grace.
His grace is enough.
His grace is why I sing.
His power made perfect in weakness.
I'm safe under His wings.

<u>Thank you</u>

May of 2010
You are my Healer.
You are my Savior.
You are my Provider.

You are my Protector.
You have saved me.
You heal my brokenness.
You have given me joy.
You love me-even when I'm a mess.
Thank you for who you are.
Thank you for what you do.
Thanks for making my heart new.
Hear my heart because thank you is not enough.
Thank you for the cross.
Thank you for never leaving
Thank you for your love.
Thank you, King of Kings,
<u>Live by the Spirit</u>
There's a battle inside me-
Waging war on my mind.
One voice brings life and peace
The other will just bind.
My flesh calls out to be fed.
My spirit has a smaller voice.
Which one will I listen to?
Pick the spirit and find joy.
Get rid of the flesh.
Live by the Spirit.
The spirit gives life but the flesh-death.
Live by the Spirit.
It's not an easy battle
But it's worth the sweat.
My God is with me.
He is my safety net.
He will help if I let...Him
The power over sin was not free.

A high price was paid at Calvary.

==========================================

Care For You

6-4-10

Don't pretend all is okay.
When you're hurting inside.
That smile is fake-
Under a mask you hide.
When asked how you were
You said "fine" and lied.
Open your heart wide.
There's someone in whom you can confide.
Don't keep sin in the dark.
Reach out.
Tell someone you trust.
Freedom is found on that route.

I Am More

6-7-10

I am a teacher.
I am a friend.
I am a daughter and a sister too.
I help hearts to mend.
I am a selfish person.
I do wrong things.
I am a musician.
I am one who sings.
I am more than they see.
I am more than how I see me.
I am more than what I do.
I am more because of who You are in me.

I am a woman.
I am a daughter of the King.
I am loved by Him.
I am souring on eagle's wings.

———————————————————

Your Glory

2010
Getting out of bed is hard.
But I say "Good morning.
I love you Lord."
Because each day is a gift.
All for Your glory
And not my own.
I live my life
For an audience of One.
No longer consumed with
Others' opinions.
They can hate me or
Treat me wrong.
Inside I want to be noticed.
I want a thank you.
But great's my reward
On the other side.

==============================

Never Divorce You

10-10-10
People may leave you.
People will disappoint.
They may take all you got
And break your heart.
I'll never divorce you.

My love will always flow.
Nothing you do will make me go.
Don't fear. I'm always yours.
I hold you when you cry.
Every tear I keep.
I feel every pain.
My compassion will never cease.
A spouse may say goodbye.
Their love may end.
But my love is unending.
I could never let you go.
I'll never divorce you.
My love will always flow.
Nothing you do will make me go
Don't fear. I'm always yours.

My Ideal Man

(written as a teenager)

My ideal man is sweet and gentle.
He is not jealous of other men.
His personality is very pleasant.
He knows how to make me laugh.
My ideal man knows and loves God.
His friends influence him in a godly way.
He refuses to have sex until
We are married.
My ideal man treats me with respect.
He loves me even through my weaknesses.
Our relationship is a commitment.
We have a relationship, not just a date.
My ideal man cherishes me
No matter what.
He holds my hand and

Protects me in the storms.
This is my ideal man.
One day God will lead him to me.
But until then, I will keep
Trusting God in all I do.

<u>Come Up Higher</u>

You see pain.
You see disdain.
But I see value
And I see a new you.
You see brokenness.
I see how to draw you close.
You feel depressed.
(I feel it too) But I give you a hope dose.
Come up higher.
See my perspective.
Know it'll be all right
Because I'm in the light.
I'm the light
And I'll make it all right.
It'll be such a sight.
Just hold on tight
To me.
I see a bright future.
I see hope.
I see a new day dawning for you.
I see us together forever.
All tears wiped away
And all fear disappears
Come see what I see
Come be with Me

====================

Love All

7-8-16

Hate
I hate that word.
We need to love.
Love all in the world.
Put away your pride
More like-kill it
Do you want to be remembered this way?
Killing others-then you put into a pit?
I don't understand
That depth of hate.
Jesus is the answer.
Life is through the narrow gate.
No matter the color,
Religion, or race
We all bleed red.
I love and give you grace.
The battle is here.
Spirit realm is real.
Put on the armor of God.
Pray. Don't sit still.

Don't wait

3-9-19

You hurt.
The words sink deep.
It feels hopeless.
Who is this person I'm with?
Don't wait.
The time is now.

Tomorrow may be too late.
Don't worry about how.
Ask for help.
Don't wait.
You're run down.
What you do is networking.
What's wrong with your body?
So tired of sick and tired.
With each passing day
You get smaller and smaller.
The abuse gets bigger.
You matter, my friend.
They hurt you bad.
You want vengeance.
It's not fair.
Because of them, life seems like it's over.
Tell that person how you feel.
We aren't guaranteed more days.
This could be your last chance.
Love on them.

---

Daily Blessings

11-2014
In the morning I thanked the Lord
For I woke up to another day.
Someone didn't get that chance.
Then I thanked the Lord that I can walk to the bathroom.
Someone can't walk today.
Someone is so sick they can't even get out of bed.
I'm thankful for a warm house for someone lives on the streets.
Then I gave thanks I could pee

For someone can't go that easily.
I walk into my kitchen filled with food
And gave thanks that I can nourish my body.
Then I thank God for hot water to shower.
Someone bathes in a cold river or not at all.
I turn to my closet full of clothes
And give thanks- for someone only has 1 or 2 old outfits.
I turn to my Bible to hear from the Lord.
Some people haven't heard of Jesus or have a Bible.
Someone can't see physically or maybe spiritually.
As I fix my hair I'm reminded
That some people have lost all their hair from illness.
15 things already and I know I missed some
And I haven't even left the house yet.
I turn off the light and give thanks-
For someone had their electricity turned off due to finances.
I get into my car and give thanks-
I've heard it said that if you have a car and some change, you are in the top 8% richest in the world.
I give thanks that it starts-
Because someone is stuck on the side of the road today.
I give thanks for music and prayer
To start my day.
Someone has no access to music and doesn't know God.
I get to work tired and worn out
But I have a job.
Someone is hurting financially with no job- so I give thanks.
I am greeted by friendly coworkers
And so I give thanks.
I start to care for little ones and give thanks.
Someone detests their job and finds no purpose in it.
My coworker needs someone to listen to her.

I listen and give thanks that I can hear and help someone.

I work on my lesson plans and give thanks that I can write and type.

Someone has no hands or hasn't been taught to write.

I eat and drink-giving thanks for clean water.

Someone in Africa spends half their day fetching water and it's not even clean.

I teach my kids at work-

Thankful for the opportunity.

I give thanks God entrusts them to me.

I give thanks for another safe, successful work day.

As I step outside into the cold, I'm not a fan

But I give thanks because I have warm clothing and a coat.

Someone nearby doesn't.

I pull up to the store

Wishing I could go put my feet up.

But I give thanks that I have money and don't have to grow my own food or make my own clothes.

Finally, I'm home and put up the groceries-thankful for the ability to do it.

I put my feet up and check my facebook-thankful for a phone and computer.

Some people can't afford such luxuries. (They are luxuries.)

I pull up to the drive-thru-thankful for others cooking and serving me.

(I've done this kind of work. It's not real fun so be gracious.)

I pull into my church parking lot-thankful for the freedom we enjoy in this country.

Someone is a believer in secret and could be persecuted if caught.

I enjoy being with Christ, hearing his word, and worshipping.

Meanwhile, someone is worshipping a false God, believing they are right in their faith. Or they are home bound- so they have no way to get to church.

I have a soul talk with a friend-

Thankful for friends that share life and care about me.

I go home and prepare for my next workday- grateful for something to prepare for.

I read a good book-thankful that I can read.

Many people never learned to read and are handicapped in their learning and their career.

I say goodnight to my room mate.

Someone is alone and grieving the death of a loved one.

Someone hasn't heard someone say they love them in a long time.

This is just one possible day.

What will we focus on?

Will we complain because life is not meeting up to what we want?

Or will we give thanks in everything?

Will we see and not take all the "small things" for granted?

——————————————————-

<u>Chapter 4 joy questions</u>

1. Are you choosing joy?
2. Which dog are you feeding more? (flesh or spirit)
3. What are your dreams? Write them.

Pick one goal and work on it for 5 hours a week.

1. Do you have a word from God to get you through this difficult season?

How to get a word from God: read the Bible

Ask Him for a word- Pay attention what comes to your mind. It could be a picture, scripture, phrase, or even just one word. If it lines up with the Bible, chances are that God just talked to you.

1. Pick 3-5 of my poems that really resonate with you. Read them on a regular basis if they encourage you.

Ex: Joy

Worship. example: I love you Lord

Receiving ex: Ask and receive

Thoughts about yourself ex: so beautiful, I think, mirror image)

# Appendix 1

How to receive Christ

I was taught this as a child, and I still remember and hold to it.

Say a prayer covering these four things:

Confess- confess your sin to God. Tell Him you've messed up.

Repent- "I'm sorry Lord. Please forgive me and help me change."

Believe- Believe that Jesus is Lord. Believe that He died and rose again for your sin and eternal life.

Romans 3:23 All have sinned and fallen short of the glory of God.

6:23 - The wages of sin is death but the gift of God is eternal life in Jesus Christ our Lord.

10:9-10

Receive his gift of eternity and forever relationship with Him. He wants to be closer to you than you can imagine but you've got to let Him. He's my Best friend and no one could ever take His place in my life. My journey started with him as a little girl in a back church pew. I still remember the cleansing and the hope even though I was only a little girl. Remember it's about relationship with Him not just all the rules and regulations. Get a Bible. Find a church. Hang out with believers.

Welcome to the family! I'd love to hear about your entering God's family. Please let me know through my wordpress account mentioned at the beginning of the book.

God loves you.

Blessings.

The last few weeks I have been thinking about the conclusion and I was stumped. How can I sum this all up? Then I talked with my coach and he gave me clarity. I want to just be candid and share my heart. As I write these words, I have had almost four good months. I now have more good days than bad. It's been a while since that' s happened. It'll happen for you too. God's provided every step of the way-from places to live and work, financial help, and to emotional support. I'm free and look forward to the future. For I know, it is good. For my God, Jesus Christ, is very good.

Before that for a year, I was not well. I had just left my ex -husband. Then we were trying to make it work, but it was to no avail. I had hope until September when I was broken in a way I've never experienced before. I felt betrayed deeper than ever before. I got more depressed than I think I'd ever been to that point. A month later we decided it was over. In November he treated me badly as we talked about settling the divorce assets. That was one of my most broken nights. I had a lot of broken nights. At night, we can't distract ourselves. The pain is there with us. I had three months where I got 3-4 hours of sleep a night. That does not work with me very well. I am a woman that needs my sleep! But God brought me through. I went to work even though I was exhausted. His grace was more than enough.

I love Christmas, but that Christmas was painful. I reached out to friends and family, and they helped me. The thing about Christmas is that it highlights how you already feel. If you are joyful, you'll be super joyful. If you are sad, you're sadness will be multiplied. It makes Christmas either super great or super painful. December 14 I finally had the courage to go to the lawyer. It was a very painful and hard step. Looking back, it's one of the best things I'd ever done for myself. I was standing up for myself and my mental health. I was saying "no more"!

January through March were the most painful. I found out something that hurt me to the core and I kept going by his house, which just prolonged and exasperated my already broken heart. Ladies and gentlemen, don't do that. I'd never felt so much anger. It scared me and I sought help. Reach out for help, friend. You can't do this alone. Trust me. There are people that want to help and that love you, but you must make your needs known.

You may be in the yuck and pain right now. But I promise, it will pass. And as a believer, God will use it for good in your life. He's amazing how He does that. Restoration is around the corner. You'll get through. Just never give up hope.

Thinking back to what I would've told myself months ago, this is what I would've said:

1. This won't be forever. There will come a day where there's more good days than bad days. And you will rejoice.
2. Do everything you can to reach toward healing. Your heart is very important.
3. When you cry, God cries with you. He may feel far away, but

He is actual quite close. The Bible says He is near to the broken hearted. Draw near to Him.

4. You're doing better than you think. Love yourself. Take it day by day or even hour by hour if you need to.
5. Grieving is hard, exhausting work. Give yourself a break.
6. Get a Word from God and remember what He said. The lies bombarding your mind are bogus. Trash those evil lies.
7. God is not judging you, so stop judging yourself and worrying about what others think.
8. Find people that will just sit and be with you. There's so much comfort in that. But also realize that people are just people. They can't meet all your needs, but God can. People will let you down in this time. Try not to be hurt or disappointed.
9. Journal. It will help. Trust me.
10. Reach out. Don't be a recluse right now. That's how you will be beat. You need other people.
11. There's hope for the future. It may feel like the end, but it's actually a new beginning to your life.
12. You are loved. You are loved. You are loved. Your feelings saying you aren't loved are lies. Reject those lies. Receive love from God and others.
13. Circumstances nor people define you. God alone does. Quit giving them that power. You're not a big D for divorcee or W for widow.... You're a child of the Most High God.
14. You're strong. You can do this. You will survive and thrive. Speak life.
15. It will be okay. This is only temporary pain. Yes, you're life will never be the same. But beautiful flowers come after rain and winter seasons.
16. More self care! Do things you love. You matter and you're important.
17. What others do to hurt you is not a reflection of you. It's a

reflection of them. Hurt people hurt people.

18. Tell people what you need. They can't read minds. But also be careful who you talk to. Make sure they are trustworthy people.
19. You don't need the addiction or bad ways of coping. You don't need the relationship, shopping, food, TV, excessive sleep, drugs, alcohol...God can meet those needs much better. Try turning to Him instead and ask for help from Him. But also, no condemnation in Christ if you turn to these things. I only hope better for you.
20. You will see who your real friends are. It's okay. Let go what needs to be let go of. Your timing is okay. Just let go. You'll be better off for it.

I sincerely hope this book has helped you. God had you on His mind when He put this book into my heart in the fall and winter months where I endured so much emotional pain. (I think the worst I have felt to date.) When He woke me up early on the weekends with words pouring out onto the pages. When I even started writing poems as a teenager. He knew about you on this day reading these words. Rest assured. He knows. I believe He drew you to this book. If it helped you, share it with someone else who needs hope on the path to restoration. There's always hope. Always. Remember that, friends. God bless you on your personal path to restoration.

Acknowledgements

Thank you, Victoria Garmonia, for doing my book editing for me.

Thank you to my book coach, Jed Jurchenko.

Thank you, Self Publishing School, for teaching me how to do this and giving me the help and tools I needed... Look them up if you need help writing a book.

## About the Author

Sarah Lowe has lived in the Dallas Forth Worth area of Texas all her life. She has eight nieces and nephews and has worked with children for ten years. Music, children, and helping others are some of her passions. She has written poems and songs since teenagehood. She awaits the day when she has her own family and children.

# Also by Sarah Lowe

The Path to Restoration

www.ingramcontent.com/pod-product-compliance
Lightning Source LLC
LaVergne TN
LVHW091124150826
845673LV00002B/961

* 9 7 9 8 2 3 0 6 8 3 9 6 4 *